Honeybees

Place Value

Kristy Stark, M.A.Ed.

Consultant

Lorrie McConnell, M.A.
Professional Development Specialist TK–12
Moreno Valley USD, CA

Publishing Credits

Rachelle Cracchiolo, M.S.Ed., *Publisher*
Conni Medina, M.A.Ed., *Managing Editor*
Dona Herweck Rice, *Series Developer*
Emily R. Smith, M.A.Ed., *Series Developer*
Diana Kenney, M.A.Ed., NBCT, *Project Manager*
June Kikuchi, *Content Director*
Stacy Monsman, M.A., *Editor*
Michelle Jovin, M.A., *Assistant Editor*
Fabiola Sepulveda, *Graphic Designer*

Image Credits: p.9 (top) Lois Elvey/Stockimo/Alamy; p.27 A Katz/Shutterstock; all other images from iStock and/or Shutterstock.

Library of Congress Cataloging-in-Publication Data

Names: Stark, Kristy, author.
Title: Honeybees / Kristy Stark.
Description: Huntington Beach, CA : Teacher Created Materials, [2018] |
    Series: Amazing animals | Audience: K to grade 3. | Includes index. |
    Identifiers: LCCN 2017049047 (print) | LCCN 2017050269 (ebook) | ISBN
    9781480759923 (eBook) | ISBN 9781425857424 (pbk.)
Subjects: LCSH: Honeybee--Juvenile literature.
Classification: LCC QL737.U56 (ebook) | LCC QL737.U56 S7345 2018 (print) |
    DDC 595.79/9--dc23
LC record available at https://lccn.loc.gov/2017049047

Teacher Created Materials
5301 Oceanus Drive
Huntington Beach, CA 92649-1030
http://www.tcmpub.com

ISBN 978-1-4258-5742-4
© 2018 Teacher Created Materials, Inc.
Printed in China
Nordica.022018.CA21701404

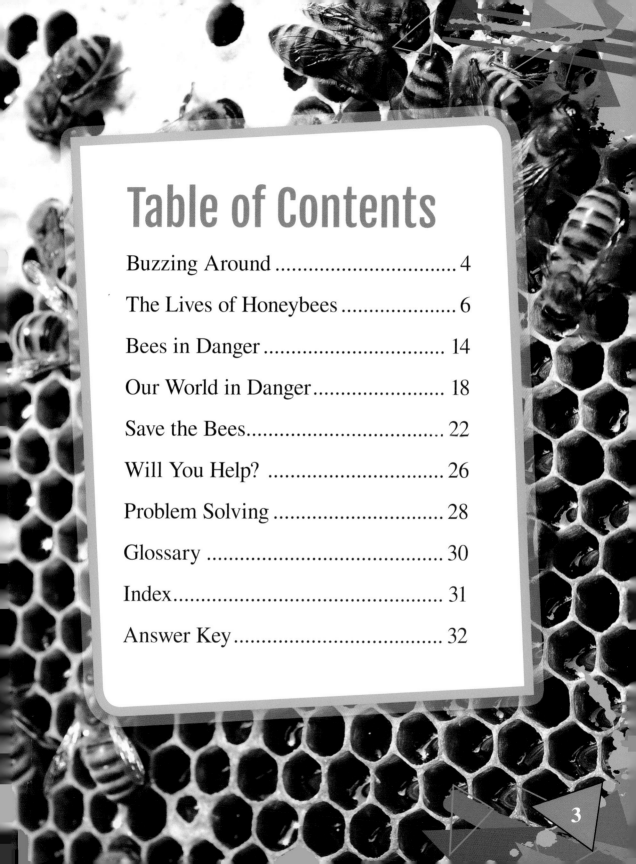

Table of Contents

Buzzing Around

Have you ever watched a bee fly? You may have seen bees buzzing around plants and flowers. Did you wonder what the bees were doing?

You may think bees fly around so they can sting people. But that is not true. Bees will only sting if they are scared or bothered.

Honeybees would rather do their jobs than sting people. Their jobs are very important.

The Lives of Honeybees

bee hive

One job that honeybees have is to build their homes. But they do not have to do it alone. Honeybees live in big groups called **colonies**. Colonies work together to build their homes. These homes are called hives. Most of the time, bees build their hives in trees.

The honey that people buy in stores comes from bee farms. The bees on farms do not build their hives in trees like wild honeybees do. The bees on farms live in big boxes that are used as their hives.

Bees on farms use boxes like these as their hives.

Look at the picture below. Find the number of honeybees.

Which of the following show the number of bees in the picture?

A. ▱▱▱▱▱▱▱
B. ▱▱▱▱▱▱▱
C. ▱▱▱▱▱▱▱▱▱

Honeybees have another job. They make honey from nectar. Nectar is a sweet juice found in flowers. Bees love the taste. They spend their days searching for nectar. One bee may drink nectar from hundreds and hundreds of flowers each day!

Honeybees use their long tongues to drink nectar from flowers. When they drink their fill, they go back to their hives. Once there, they spit into other bees' mouths. These bees chew the nectar for about 30 minutes. Then, they spit it into the honeycomb part of the hive.

bees in a honeycomb

A honeybee uses its tongue to suck up nectar from flowers.

These honeybees dry honey in a honeycomb.

The next step is to dry the nectar. Nectar will dry on its own. But honeybees can speed up the **process**. They begin by flapping their wings very quickly. Bees can flap their wings close to two hundred times per second! Their wings act like little fans. The nectar becomes thick, smooth honey when it dries.

Honeybees can flap their wings close to two hundred times each second. Which of the following shows the number closest to two hundred?

A.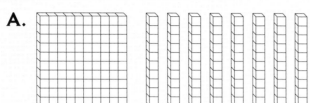

B.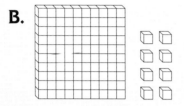

C.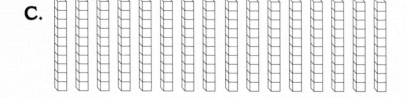

Helping Plants

Honeybees make honey that people eat. But that is not all they do. Bees help flowers, too. Flowers have a dust called pollen. It sticks to bees when they land. Bees move pollen from flower to flower when they drink nectar. This process is called **pollination**. It helps flowers make seeds to grow new plants.

This bee is covered in pollen.

There are 10 fruit trees. Each tree has 10 honeybees drinking nectar from its flowers.

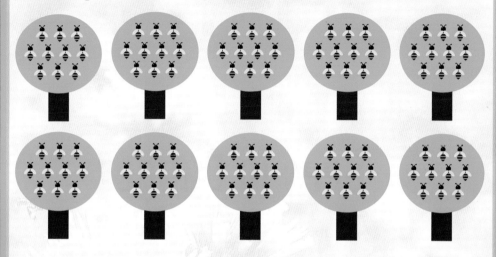

1. Which of these shows the number of bees on 1 tree?

2. Which of these shows the number of bees on all the fruit trees?

A. ▭

B. ▦

C. ▱▱▱▱▱▱▱▱▱▱

A. ▭

B. ▦

C. ▱▱▱▱▱▱▱▱▱▱

Bees in Danger

Honeybees help plants and animals. Many animals eat the plants that bees help grow. These animals **depend** on bees. Without bees, their lives would change.

But bees are in danger. They are dying from **chemicals** that are used to kill bugs. Farmers want to keep bugs from eating their **crops**. The chemicals they spray to kill those bugs can hurt bees, too.

Bees pollinate many crops, including lemon trees.

Two farmers spray chemicals on plants to kill bugs.

If honeybees keep dying, they may become **extinct**. Then, there will be no more honey. Crops will not be pollinated. Without bees, many plants will die.

Fruit and nut trees will not grow foods for us to eat. There will be no more almonds. Apples and peaches will stop growing, too. People will not get to eat many of the foods they love.

Two boys enjoy fruit.

The trees that grow these fruits all need to be pollinated.

Our World in Danger

Honeybees **affect** many things around them. Bees are small insects. But they play a big role in Earth's **food chain**.

Without bees, **creatures** such as squirrels and mice will not have berries and seeds for food. These small animals will die without food.

LET'S EXPLORE MATH

1. There are 100 + 40 + 6 mice eating berries in a field. Write one number to show how many mice there are.

2. In the same field, there are 192 squirrels eating acorns. Write 192 as a total of hundreds, tens, and ones.

A honeybee carries pollen from one plant to another.

Berries grow when the plant has been pollinated.

A mouse eats the berries.

19

Small animals are food for large animals. Many large animals, such as owls and foxes, eat small animals, such as mice and squirrels. Large creatures will die without food to eat.

Bees affect many other creatures in our world. Without bees, our lives will change. Many plants will not grow. Lots of animals will die.

Foxes and owls eat mice.

A mouse eats berries.

21

Save the Bees

Bees are dying around the world, but you can help save them. Start by planting flowers that bees like. These flowers will give bees nectar.

Be sure to plant flowers that will bloom at different times of the year. That way, bees will always be able to get nectar. Bees get a lot of nectar from weeds, such as clovers. Weeds can cause other problems. But bees need them.

clover

A honeybee drinks nectar from a clover.

You can also help bees by not spraying chemicals on plants. Chemicals make bees sick. If you have bees in your yard, have an adult call a beekeeper. Beekeepers are trained to work with bees. They can get them out of your yard. Then, they can move the hive to a safe place.

A beekeeper moves a hive on a bee farm.

Large hives can have more than 50,000 honeybees.

Will You Help?

Honeybees have many big jobs. They make honey for people to eat, and they help plants grow. They help make food for many animals, too.

We will all be in trouble without honeybees. Our lives will change. But small changes can help save them. Start helping bees today. It is up to all of us to keep bees safe.

These people want farmers to stop using chemicals on crops.

NO BEES
NO Fruits
NO VEGETABLES

GIVE BEES A chance
NO GMO
NO GMOS
NO Pesticides

⚙ Problem Solving

José and Makayla have bees on their farm. First, the bees make honey. Then, they sell the honey.

1. José and Makayla have 52 hive boxes. Which of the following show 52?

A.

B.

C.

D.

2. José and Makayla add 8 more hive boxes. How many hive boxes do they have now? How do you know?

3. The bees on the farm make 108 pounds of honey in a month.

    a. Writc 108 as a total of hundreds, tens, and ones.

    b. Draw the number line below, and plot 108.

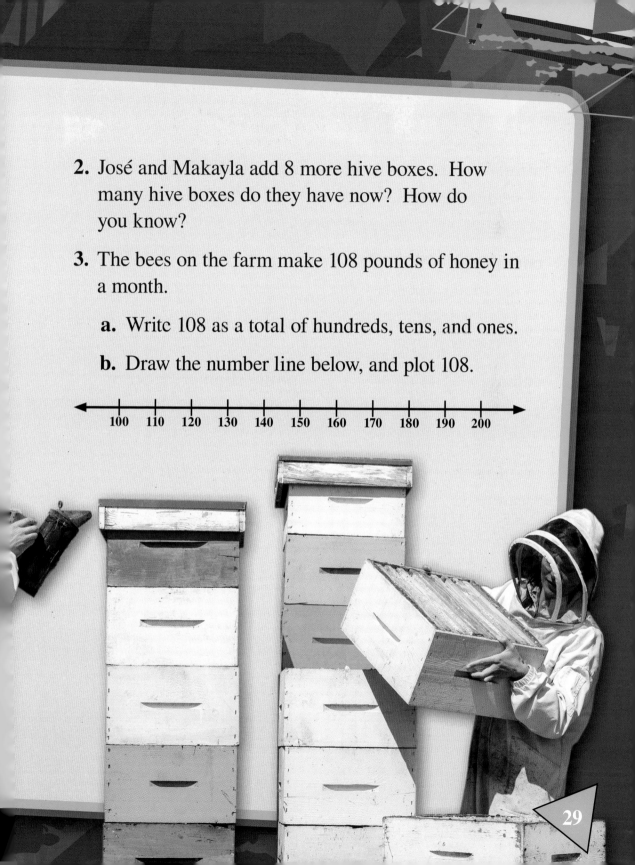

```
<───┼────┼────┼────┼────┼────┼────┼────┼────┼────┼──>
   100  110  120  130  140  150  160  170  180  190  200
```

Glossary

affect—act on a person or thing and cause it to change

chemicals—things that are made when two or more substances are mixed together

colonies—groups of similar people or things living in one place

creatures—types of animals

crops—groups of plants grown by farmers

depend—need or to count on someone or something

extinct—no longer existing in the world

food chain—a chain of events in which one type of living thing is food for another type of living thing

pollination—the act of moving pollen from one plant to another

process—a series of actions that produce something or make something happen

Index

Answer Key

Let's Explore Math

page 7:
B and C

page 11:
A

page 13:
1. A and C
2. B

page 18:
1. 146 mice
2. $100 + 90 + 2$

Problem Solving

1. A and D
2. 60 hive boxes; Answers will vary but may include $52 + 8 = 60$.
3. **a.** $100 + 0 + 8$

   b.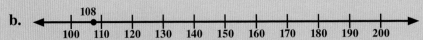